THE
THE VIRTUE MANUALS

Saints' Guides to a Flourishing Life

VIA AD VIRTUTEM

SAINTLY SKILLS FOR LIFE'S JOURNEY

The Prudence Manual: Spyridon's Guide to Wise Choices
A Practical Handbook for Cultivating Thoughtful Decision-Making and Foresight

Text by Bronwyn Finch
Illustrations by Mark Anderson

ISBN: 978-1-989647-77-6
First published 10/6/2025
Toronto, Canada

Publisher: The Evergreen Centre

Publisher's Cataloging-in-Publication Data

Finch, Bronwyn.
The Prudence Manual: Spyridon's Guide to Wise Choices | text by Bronwyn Finch ;
illustrations by Mark Anderson. — First edition.
Summary: A practical handbook using the life and wisdom of Saint Spyridon to
teach middle school readers the four essential sub-virtues of prudence—observation,
foresight, discernment, and self-correction—as a skill for sound, thoughtful decision-
making.
Identifiers: ISBN 978-1-989647-77-6
Subjects: Prudence—Juvenile literature. | Saint Spyridon—Juvenile literature.
| Virtue Ethics—Juvenile literature. | Decision Making—Juvenile literature. |
Character Education—Juvenile literature.
Classification: 248.8—dc23

The Prudence Manual:
St. Spyridon's Guide to Wise Choices

A Practical Handbook for Cultivating Thoughtful
Decision-Making and Foresight

Text by Bronwyn Finch
Illustrations by Mark Anderson

PRUDENCE - YOUR INNER COMPASS

St. Spyridon

Introduction:
Welcome to Your First Manual

Section 1:
Your Mission Brief
What is Prudence?

You're holding a powerful tool—
your first Virtue Manual.

It's not just a book to read; it's
a skill guide to help you master
Prudence, the art of making wise
choices.

Your instructor for this journey
is St. Spyridon, a historical figure
who honed this skill every day.

Get ready to read, reflect, and put
these practical skills to use.

Prudence
(noun)

Definition:

The quality of being prudent; the ability to govern and discipline oneself by the use of reason; sagacity or shrewdness in the management of affairs; skill and good judgment in the use of resources; caution or forethought as to danger or risk.

In simpler terms, it's the ability to make wise, careful, and well-thought-out decisions, especially concerning the future.

What is Prudence?

Prudence is far more than an ancient, complicated word—it's your inner superpower for astute decision-making.

It represents the cultivated ability to thoughtfully assess any given situation, anticipate potential outcomes, and then strategically select the most beneficial course of action.

Like mastering an instrument or excelling in a sport, prudence is a dynamic skill, one that deepens and strengthens with consistent application and dedicated practice.

Each deliberate choice you make reinforces this vital internal capacity.

2

How This Manual Works

This isn't a textbook you just read and forget. It's a practical handbook.

We'll explore Spyridon's Case Files—real stories from history that show Prudence in action.

Each case file highlights a specific Prudence skill, like observation or planning, and shows you the tangible results.

After seeing how St. Spyridon did it, you'll get to try it yourself with the Skill-Builder Drills. These are simple, hands-on exercises designed to help you practice what you've learned.

The goal is to move from understanding Prudence to actively using it in your daily life.

Word Origin:

The word "prudence" comes from the Old French "prudence" (meaning "prudence, discretion, wisdom"), which in turn derives from the Latin "prudentia." "Prudentia" itself is a contraction of "providentia," meaning "foresight, providence."

The Opposite of Prudence:

The opposite of prudence is acting without thinking—being imprudent, rash, or reckless.

It's making quick decisions without considering the consequences, jumping into situations carelessly, or ignoring the signs that a choice might lead to trouble.

While Prudence helps you plan ahead and choose wisely, its opposite can lead to unexpected problems and regret.

Why Prudence Matters: Your Essential Inner Compass

Consider your life a compelling journey. While some paths are clear, others present intricate forks, unforeseen obstacles, or subtle pitfalls.

This is precisely where Prudence becomes your essential inner compass, expertly guiding you to navigate your chosen course.

It empowers you through significant decisions—from complex social dynamics and academic strategies to personal prioritizations—allowing you to always select the path that aligns with your true well-being and aspirations.

It is vitality important to remember, Prudence, like all virtues, is not a burden enforced upon you; it is a powerful tool you choose to wield, designed to help you succeed and thrive in all aspects of your life.

The Path of Folly: Risks of Abandoning Prudence

When we abandon Prudence for folly and impulse, the path ahead becomes far less certain.

Acting on immediate urges, we often overlook potential consequences, leading to a string of regrettable decisions that could have been easily avoided.

Choosing folly means building a life on unstable ground.

Without the inner scaffolding of Prudence, you're more likely to feel overwhelmed, lose confidence, and drift through life without a clear, positive direction.

Does Practicing Prudence Mean No Fun?

Absolutely not!

Prudence isn't about avoiding enjoyment; it's about making wise choices that lead to better, more sustainable fun and fewer regrets.

It helps you consider the full picture, ensuring your fun today doesn't cause problems tomorrow.

Instead of limiting fun, prudence helps you maximize it by thinking ahead.

What is "Inner Scaffolding"?

"Inner scaffolding" refers to the strong internal support structure you build within yourself through consistently making prudent, thoughtful choices.

Prudence as an Ancient Value

Prudence was recognized as a cornerstone of wisdom in ancient philosophy, particularly by the Greeks and Romans.

Philosophers like Plato and Aristotle considered it one of the four cardinal virtues, essential for living a good and rational life.

For them, Prudence was the practical wisdom to discern the right course of action in any given situation, allowing individuals to navigate complex moral dilemmas and make decisions that led to overall well-being and a flourishing society.

Prudence as a Christian Virtue

Within Christianity, Prudence is deeply integrated as a moral virtue, often seen as the "charioteer of the virtues" because it guides all others.

Christian theology adopted and adapted ancient philosophical concepts, seeing Prudence as the intellectual virtue that helps individuals discern their true good in every circumstance and choose the right means to achieve it.

It's crucial for living a virtuous life aligned with God's will, ensuring that faith, hope, and charity are applied wisely and effectively in daily actions.

Why is "Inner scaffolding" a positive foundation?

It provides resilience and stability when facing challenges, acting as your mental backbone.

This scaffolding fosters confidence in your decisions, prevents regret, and forms a reliable, values-driven foundation for your character, enabling consistent personal growth.

Spyridon's Case Files:
Historical Lessons in Prudence

Now that you know what Prudence is, let's see it in action.

In this section, you'll open four "Case Files" from the life of St. Spyridon.

Each story is a real-world example of how he used prudence to navigate challenges and make wise choices, from his days as a shepherd to his later life as a respected leader.

As you read, pay close attention to the specific Prudence skill Spyridon demonstrates. These aren't just old tales; they're blueprints for your own journey, showing you tangible ways to develop your "inner superpower" and achieve your own "Aha!" moments.

The Shepherd's Challenge- A Life of Prudence A Demanding Calling:

In St. Spyridon's era, shepherding was no easy task. It demanded constant vigilance, not just a casual watch.

A shepherd was the sole protector of their flock against a harsh world, facing dangers that could quickly wipe out their livelihood.

Case File 1:
The Shepherd's Vigil –
Sharpening Your Observation Skill

Long before he was a famous saint, Spyridon was a simple shepherd on the island of Cyprus. In the sun-drenched, rugged hills of Roman-governed Cyprus, his life was intertwined with the demanding rhythms of the Mediterranean.

His daily existence was a masterclass in vigilance: fresh water could be scarce, sudden storms appeared without warning, and both wild animals and bandits posed constant threats. This was a challenging land that demanded constant attention, much like the ancient proverb: *"The prudent sees danger and hides himself, but the simple go on and suffer for it."* (Proverbs 22:3)

Spyridon embodied this wisdom.

10

In this untamed environment, his flock's very survival depended entirely on his acute observation skills. He didn't merely see the sky; he read the clouds' color and movement like a detailed map, predicting oncoming storms with uncanny accuracy.

He didn't just look at his sheep; he noticed a subtle limp, unusual restlessness, or scattered grazing patterns— each a vital piece of data indicating a problem that needed immediate attention. Spyridon knew precisely where the best grasses grew, where springs bubbled even in dry seasons, and the hidden dens of predators that stalked the night. He didn't simply see the world around him; he understood it deeply, deciphering its silent language.

This patient, careful gathering of information was the bedrock of all his prudent decisions,

Battling Nature and Predators:

Sheep were always vulnerable. Wild predators like wolves and jackals were a constant threat, as were human thieves.

Furthermore, shepherds had to master Cyprus's unpredictable elements: finding dwindling water in scorching summers, identifying safe pastures after torrential winter flash floods, and keenly reading subtle changes in coastal winds or mountain clouds to avert seasonal disasters.

No Room for Error:

Without modern veterinary care or reliable shelter, one sick animal could quickly devastate the entire flock.

Every decision, from choosing a grazing spot to timing a move, was critical.

A single imprudent choice could mean financial ruin or even starvation for the shepherd and their family.

allowing him to lead his flock to safety and prosperity not by chance, but by truly seeing and interpreting every detail the landscape offered.

Prudence Skill Demonstrated-
Observation & Data Gathering.

This is the fundamental skill of seeing, listening, and truly understanding a situation before you act. It's a detective's first rule: gather the evidence.

The "Aha!" Moment:

Spyridon's flock thrived not because of a miracle, but because of his skill. His wisdom came from paying attention to the small details others missed.

Integrated Wisdom Bite:

"You cannot navigate a path you have not yet seen. Look closely, for your choices begin not in the doing, but in the seeing."

Case File 2:
Protecting the Innocent
- The Skill of Foresight &
Planning

During St. Spyridon's lifetime,
drought on Cyprus wasn't just
inconvenient—it was life-
threatening. Years of little rain
left crops withered, springs dry,
and pastures turned to dust.
For a shepherd, this meant real
danger: weak, thirsty flocks
were easy prey to disease and
starvation. Drought forced
terrible choices, often ending in
dead animals, hungry families,
and whole villages on the move.
It was a harsh test of Prudence,
demanding foresight and
planning just to survive.

As a bishop, Spyridon's flock
became people, and his duty
grew greater. One year, a famine
struck. Crops failed. Panic
spread. Some starved, while
greedy traders hoarded grain
and raised prices sky-high.

Storing for Survival:

Communities
carefully stored
rainwater in
cisterns and
grain from
good harvests.

Leaders like
St. Spyridon
organized
these vital
reserves.

This foresight
created crucial
buffers against
starvation
when Cyprus's
dry seasons
inevitably hit.

Cultivating Resilience:

Farmers prudently chose drought-resistant crops like olives and grapes, which thrive in arid conditions.

They also practiced terracing, building stone walls on hillsides to create flat steps.

This captured precious rainwater, preventing runoff and allowing it to soak deep into the soil, sustaining crops through dry periods.

But Spyridon's community was spared. Why? Because he had been watchful. Months earlier, while others celebrated the harvest, he noticed the poor rainfall and the unusual warmth.

He heard whispers of trouble in distant lands. He didn't brush them off—he acted. Meeting with farmers and merchants, he prudently purchased and stored grain at fair prices while it was still available.

When the famine came, he was ready. He didn't scramble for answers or beg for help. His foresight and planning saved his people from disaster.

Prudence Skill Demonstrated:
Foresight & Strategic Planning.

This is the ability to anticipate future consequences and plan proactive steps to achieve positive outcomes or prevent negative ones. It's about thinking three steps ahead, like a chess master. As scripture wisely states, *"The plans of the diligent lead surely to abundance, but everyone who is hasty comes only to poverty."* (Proverbs 21:5)

The "Aha!" Moment:

Spyridon's foresight wasn't about predicting the future with magic; it was about using present information to prepare for what was likely to happen. He transformed fear into action.

Integrated Wisdom Bite:

"A fool plans only for today's meal. The wise one plants a seed for tomorrow's harvest."

Spyridon's Strategic Grain Reserve:

Spyridon's famine foresight was brilliant strategy: he knew grain needed protection.

He likely used underground silos, sealed tight to starve pests and preserve grain for years.

Above-ground, he'd ensure raised floors for rodents and secure walls against thieves.

These concrete methods made his community's grain a reliable lifeline.

The Power of "Tell Me More..."

When a conversation gets heated or someone is being unfair, your first instinct might be to argue back.

Instead, try Spyridon's move: 'Tell me more about why you feel that way.'

Or 'Can you explain what you mean?'

This simple question often defuses tension and unlocks hidden information, changing the entire direction of the problem.

Case File 3:
The Gift of Counsel -
Mastering Discernment & Judgment

Spyridon's reputation for profound wisdom spread far beyond his village, attracting people from all corners of Cyprus and beyond who desperately sought his counsel. They came not just for legal advice, but for clarity in their most entangled personal and spiritual struggles.

One particularly challenging case involved two brothers, Demetrius and Lysander, locked in a bitter legal dispute over their deceased father's inheritance. The case had dragged on for months, overwhelming the local courts with its complexity. Each brother presented conflicting evidence, veiled accusations, and outright distortions, making it nearly impossible to uncover the truth and find a just resolution. Frustrated and at a deadlock, the local authorities ultimately referred the seemingly intractable case to Spyridon.

When the brothers arrived, Spyridon didn't immediately delve into their legal documents or listen to their rehearsed arguments. Instead, he observed them intently, listening not only to their words but also to what lay unspoken beneath their anger and accusations.

He discerned that the core issue wasn't just about money or property; it was a deeper wound of pride, resentment, and unaddressed familial grievances. Through a series of gentle, yet incisive questions, Spyridon patiently guided each brother to look beyond their own self-interest. He helped Demetrius acknowledge his long-held jealousy, and Lysander recognize his desire for control rather than true

When a Deal Feels "Off"

Someone wants you to join their group, but something just feels 'off.' You can't quite say why.

Prudence says: Don't ignore that gut feeling. What information are you missing? What questions aren't being asked? That quiet alarm bell is data, too.

Listen to it before you commit.

The Two Sides of the Story (And the One Underneath)

"Your friend swears she's right about the project, but your other friend has a totally different version.

Instead of picking a side, pause. Ask yourself: What's the real problem they're both trying to solve?

Or what's making them so defensive?

The true issue is rarely on the surface.

fairness. He didn't lecture or condemn; he facilitated a space where they could begin to see the root causes of their own stubbornness and the corrosive effect it had on their brotherhood.

His final judgment was firm and unwavering, but delivered with profound grace and a deep understanding of human nature. He didn't just divide the assets; he prescribed a solution that required both brothers to make concessions and, more importantly, to perform acts of reconciliation.

This resolution not only settled the intricate financial and property dispute justly, satisfying the demands of the law, but also began the arduous process of healing their deeply fractured relationship.

Spyridon's counsel became a masterclass in true discernment—moving beyond superficial facts to uncover the underlying truths and using that insight to forge a wise, holistic solution.

Prudence Skill Demonstrated- Discernment & Sound Judgment.

This is the ability to weigh options, understand underlying truths, and make a firm, well-reasoned decision. It's the ability to find the heart of the problem, for *"The discerning heart seeks knowledge".* (Proverbs 15:14)

The "Aha!" Moment:

Spyridon showed that true judgment isn't about finding a winner or a loser, but about revealing the core truth and using it to guide a wise resolution.

Integrated Wisdom Bite:

"True judgment is not in finding a winner, but in helping all parties find the truth."

When Reserves Vanish

Remember famine? What if an official claimed grain vanished, or upstream villages diverted rivers?

Spyridon's judgment traced grain paths, river flows, seeking a missing seal or new ditch.

He discerned disaster from deceit, ensuring fairness.

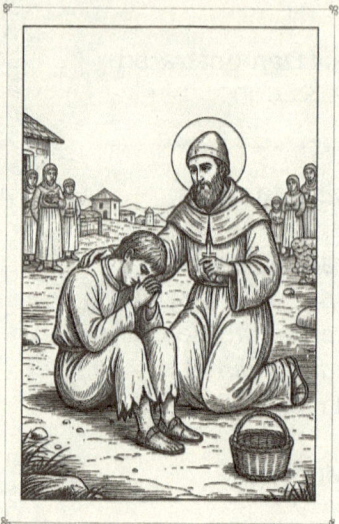

THE VIRTUE MANUALS · SAINTLY SKILLS FOR LIFE'S JOURNEY

Case File 4:

Learning from Mistakes
– The Skill of Adaptation & Correction

Perfection is never the true goal of Prudence; instead, it's the continuous journey of growth and striving to be better. To believe we must be flawless in every decision often leads to disillusionment and discouragement, making us afraid to act at all.

Prudence teaches us that getting better is always achievable, even when we stumble. This virtue also wisely reminds us that we don't have to invent every solution ourselves.

Sometimes, the most prudent path is to humbly learn from those who came before us, following the established wisdom of tradition—not simply for the sake of tradition itself, or to be seen as "good," but because it represents a

Sometimes, even with our best effort, judgment falters, or instinct leads us astray. A quick decision might backfire, or a plan may unexpectedly fail. But these moments are not reasons to abandon the virtue of prudence. Instead, they are vital opportunities for growth. Every misstep becomes a lesson, sharpening our ability to reflect, adapt, and refine our inner compass for the next decision. Prudence teaches us resilience, urging us to learn from every experience and keep striving for wiser paths.

When the Flock Falls III

Imagine a shepherd, perhaps even a young Spyridon, who misjudged a new pasture—it seemed green, but hidden within were plants that sickened his sheep.

Disaster strikes: a disease spreads.

Does he just watch his flock suffer, blaming bad luck? No.

Prudence demands swift action.

He would have to immediately own the mistake, isolate the sick, move the healthy to new, safer ground, and frantically seek

vast library of time-tested best practices and accumulated wisdom. As scripture guides us, *"Where there is no guidance, a people falls, but in an abundance of counselors there is safety."* (Proverbs 11:14)

Even St. Spyridon, our guide in prudence, exemplified this learning process. A story from his life tells of a time when, as a father figure to his community, he initially delivered a harsh judgment upon a young boy caught stealing.

In his righteous zeal to teach the boy a severe lesson and protect the community's resources, Spyridon acted swiftly. However, in that moment, he momentarily overlooked a crucial component of profound prudence: mercy, tempered with justice. He wanted to correct the wrong, but his method lacked the full balance of wisdom.

Yet, Spyridon was also a man of deep humility and reflection.

22

After witnessing the young boy's genuine remorse and fear, he took the time to carefully reconsider his own actions and the outcome he had produced. He realized that while his initial decision was well-intentioned—aimed at upholding order and deterring crime—it wasn't the wisest or most holistic path forward for that particular individual.

With profound humility, he released the boy from the severe punishment, choosing instead to offer direct guidance, support, and a path toward rehabilitation. He adapted his approach, demonstrating that sometimes, a less-than-perfect initial choice can, through reflection and self-correction, lead to a far greater and more meaningful lesson for everyone involved—the boy, the community, and even Spyridon himself.

This ability to learn, adapt, and correct course is a cornerstone of true prudence.

remedies—perhaps a specific herb from an elder, or a new water source.

This isn't about avoiding error, but having the courage and judgment to face it head-on, learn, and fight to save what remains.

Remember: Pride can be Prudence's greatest enemy. It makes us cling to flawed decisions, refusing to re-evaluate or admit error.

True prudence requires the humility to set pride aside, honestly assess outcomes, and courageously choose a better path forward.

The Strength of Humility

Humility isn't about thinking less of yourself; it's about thinking of yourself less often.

For Prudence, it's the superpower that lets you admit: 'I might be wrong,' or 'I need help.'

This strength opens you to new information, allows you to learn from mistakes, and keeps your inner compass pointing towards the wisest path, free from the blind spots of pride.

Prudence Skill Demonstrated: Self-Correction & Adaptability.

This is the vital capacity to reflect deeply on the outcomes of your actions, to genuinely learn from every experience—whether positive or challenging—and to humbly adjust your strategy moving forward.

It's the profound strength to admit when an initial choice wasn't the wisest, accepting imperfections in the process.

More importantly, it's the courage to actively get back on the right path, making conscious adjustments and always aiming to continuously improve and fine-tune your "inner navigation system."

This skill is fundamental to continuously building your inner scaffolding.

The "Aha!" Moment:

Spyridon's humility in correcting his own initial judgment reveals a profound truth: Prudence isn't about being perfectly right every single time.

Instead, it's about the ongoing process of learning, adapting, and growing.

His example shows us that the power of Prudence lies in our ability to critically review our decisions, course-correct when necessary, and thereby become stronger, wiser, and more resilient with every step.

Integrated Wisdom Bite:

"A path is made by walking, not by knowing. Learn from every stumble, and the path will become clearer."

The Art of Being Resourceful

Make the most of what you have, especially when things go wrong.

When the expected solution isn't there, Prudence, fueled by the practice of being resourceful, asks: 'What else can I use? Who else can help?'

It's the insight to discern possibilities where others perceive only obstacles.

THE VIRTUE MANUALS · SAINTLY SKILLS FOR LIFE'S JOURNEY

Your Prudence Toolkit
More Than One Tool

You've now walked alongside St. Spyridon through four powerful case studies, observing Prudence in action. Just like a skilled carpenter has many types of screwdrivers—from a precise Phillips head to a powerful ratchet—Prudence isn't just one single skill. It's a master virtue made up of many smaller, specialized "tools" or "sub-virtues" that work together.

Spyridon showed us how to sharpen our observation, plan ahead, use sound judgment, and even correct our mistakes. But there are many more facets to this amazing inner compass.

Here are some of the essential "tools" within the virtue of Prudence, for you to reflect upon and cultivate in your own life's journey:

Observation: The skill of seeing and listening closely. *"The wise man has his eyes in his head..."*
(Ecclesiastes 2:14)

Ancient Wisdom in Action

Many of these 'prudence tools' were highly valued long before St. Spyridon's time. Ancient Greek and Roman thinkers also praised qualities like Foresight in their generals, Circumspection in their leaders, and Deliberation in their councils. They understood that carefully weighing all choices and anticipating outcomes wasn't just 'good'; it was essential for success in battle, governance, and daily life.

This shows Prudence is a timeless guide for wise living.

Foresight: Anticipating consequences and planning ahead. *"A prudent man foresees evil and hides himself..."* (Proverbs 22:3)

Discernment: Seeing the truth beneath the surface. *"The spiritual man discerns all things..."* (1 Corinthians 2:15)

Sound Judgment: Making firm, well-reasoned decisions. *"Do not judge by appearances, but judge with right judgment."* (John 7:24)

Self-Correction: Learning from mistakes and adjusting course. *"A just man falls seven times and rises again..."* (Proverbs 24:16)

Circumspection: Carefully considering all circumstances. *"Look carefully then how you walk, not as unwise but as wise."* (Ephesians 5:15)

Docility: Being open to learning from others. *"Listen to advice and accept instruction, that you may gain wisdom in the future."* (Proverbs 19:20)

Caution: Being aware of potential dangers. *"Be sober-minded; be watchful. Your adversary the devil prowls around..."* (1 Peter 5:8)

Resourcefulness: Finding clever ways to solve problems. *"Go to the ant, you sluggard; consider its ways and be wise!"* (Proverbs 6:6)

Deliberation: Thoughtfully weighing all options before acting. *"The heart of the righteous ponders how to answer..."* (Proverbs 15:28)

Saints Who Mastered Prudence

St. Spyridon isn't the only saint who demonstrated these Prudence tools. Think of St. Thomas Aquinas, known for his deep Deliberation and Discernment in complex theological questions. Or St. Benedict, whose wise Rule for monks demanded Circumspection and Docility from his followers, ensuring peace and spiritual growth. These holy figures, in their own unique ways, show us how versatile and powerful the sub-virtues of prudence truly are.

Counsel – St. Benedict Listens First

When St. Benedict founded his monasteries (500s AD), he didn't just rush into making rules.

He sought counsel from Scripture, prayer, and trusted brothers.

His careful "map-reading" gave the Church the Rule of St. Benedict, still guiding monks today.

The Three Steps of the Prudent Mind
The 3-Step Quick Hack

Prudence isn't just one thing; it's a three-step process your mind follows to make a wise choice. Think of it like a pilot navigating a plane:

Step 1: Counsel (The Map-Reading Phase)

What it is: The art of taking counsel or deliberation. This means gathering all the necessary facts and considering all possible ways to act.

St. Spyridon in Action: When the famine hit (Case File 2), his counsel involved asking: What is the situation (poor rain)? What are my options (store grain, ignore, buy later)? What do others say?

Your Skill: Observation (Case 1) and Seeking Wisdom (asking a trusted adult). You cannot choose the right path if you haven't seen the whole map.

Step 2: Judgment (The Compass-Setting Phase)

What it is: The moment of Judgment. After you've considered all the facts, you must weigh them, discard the foolish options, and decide which path is truly the best.

St. Spyridon in Action: When settling the brothers' dispute (Case File 3), his judgment wasn't based just on the law, but on discerning the root cause (pride and greed). He set the moral compass.

Your Skill: Discernment & Clarity. This step is about seeing things as they are, not as you wish them to be. Ask yourself:

- Is this choice honest? Does it align with my values?

- Is this choice just? Does it harm anyone else?

Is this choice future-proof? Will I regret this in a week, a year, or ten years?

Judgment – St. Augustine's Big Choice

Before becoming a saint, Augustine lived for pleasure and success.

But when faced with the truth of Christ, he judged that following God was worth more than worldly glory.

His "compass-setting" decision made him one of the Church's greatest teachers.

31

Command – St. Francis of Assisi Acts

St. Francis didn't just talk about living simply—he commanded himself to do it.

He gave away his wealth and lived among the poor, showing courage to follow Christ's call.

His "taking off" step inspired thousands to do the same.

The Three Steps of the Prudent Mind
The 3-Step Quick Hack (cont.)

Step 3: Command (The Taking-Off Phase)

What it is: The Command or Execution phase. Prudence is useless if you don't act on your good judgment. This is taking the final step to make the choice and seeing it through.

St. Spyridon in Action: He didn't just think about storing grain; he commanded (acted) on that decision and stored it. He then had to adapt (Case 4) his Command if the initial action was flawed.

Your Skill: Foresight (Case 2) and Self-Correction (Case 4). This step requires courage. You must commit to the wise choice, even when it's unpopular.

The Timeless Root of Prudence

The three steps of Prudence—**Counsel**, **Judgment**, and **Command**—are not modern self-help tips; they are the bedrock of Western wisdom. Rooted in the works of classical thinkers like Aristotle (who called it *Phronēsis*) and cemented in Christian thought by figures like Thomas Aquinas, Prudence was held as the "charioteer of the virtues," guiding all others. By employing this framework, you are following a continuous, time-tested tradition of careful decision-making practiced by moral leaders across two millennia, from St. Spyridon to the present day.

In our current age of impulse and fleeting trends, this classic methodology becomes your essential conservative skill. It insists on slow, deliberate thought over quick reactions, securing your choices not in temporary societal whims but in timeless truth. Prudence ultimately protects and preserves your character, helping you build a life of foresight and virtue that stands firm against the shifting sands of culture.

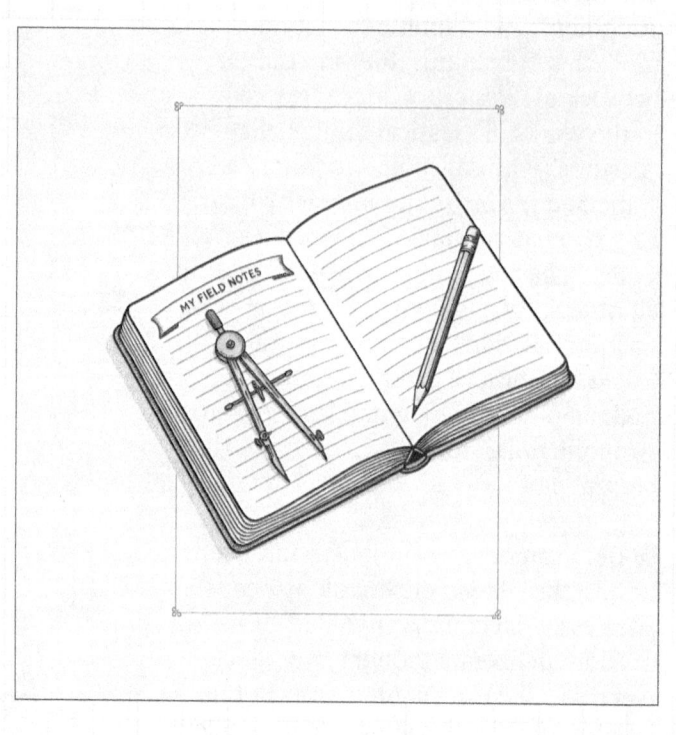

Section 4:

Your Prudence Practice Handbook

What Prudence Really Looks Like (Today)

Prudence is your inner GPS. Just like Spyridon expertly guided his flock, you can master the skill of choosing your route through decisions carefully, avoiding wrong turns, and reaching your true goals safely and wisely. It's the art of thinking before you act, not merely reacting to what's happening around you. Along this journey, you will fail, you will misjudge, and at times, you might even make the same mistakes again.

But these moments are not roadblocks; they are opportunities. Prudence empowers you to learn from every misstep, look at problems in a different light, and consistently find new, better ways to discover and arrive at the destination that is truly meant for you.

Don't Overthink It, Just Start

Feeling overwhelmed by 'all the options' for a drill? Don't let perfect be the enemy of good.

Pick just one small decision for Consequence Mapping.

Observe or read about your favorite wise person.

The goal isn't a perfect answer, but simply to start practicing. Tiny steps build big habits.

Prudence Skill-Builder Drills

These are your hands-on exercises. Try one this week and see what happens.

The "Pause & Predict" Drill:

Before you make a quick decision—like replying to a text message, sharing a post, or saying "yes" to an invitation—try this.

Pause for 5 seconds. In your mind, quickly predict 2-3 possible outcomes of your immediate action. This short pause gives your brain a chance to engage its Prudence superpower.

Consequence Mapping:

Pick one decision you need to make this week. It could be something big like choosing a club to join or small like how to spend your free afternoon. On a piece of paper, map out two different choices.

For each choice, list a few possible short-term consequences and a few long-term consequences. Which path seems wisest?

Wisdom Seekers:

Think about a person in your life you consider truly wise. This could be a parent, a teacher, a coach, or a friend. This week, simply observe how they make decisions. Do they ask a lot of questions? Do they take their time to respond? What "prudent steps" do they seem to take?

The Decision Debrief:

After you've made a decision, whether it turned out good or bad, take a moment to reflect. This is how you learn and get better.

Ask yourself: What was my goal? What did I do? What worked well? What didn't go as planned? What will I do differently next time to use my Prudence skill even better?

Why Write It Down?

You might think you can do these drills in your head. But actually writing down your predictions, consequences, or debrief notes makes a huge difference.

It forces clarity, helps you remember, and gives you a clear record of your prudence journey.

Don't skip the pen and paper!

THE VIRTUE MANUALS - SAINTLY SKILLS FOR LIFE'S JOURNEY

Your Prudence Reserve

Keep these thoughts in mind when you need a boost.

"The prudent person foresees the difficulties of the moment and guards himself; the foolish one goes blindly on and suffers." — St. Spyridon's wisdom, paraphrased

"Be not wise in your own eyes; fear the Lord and turn away from evil." — Proverbs 3:7

"If any of you lacks wisdom, let him ask God, who gives generously to all without finding fault, and it will be given to him." — James 1:5

"Look carefully then how you walk, not as unwise but as wise, making the best use of the time, because the days are evil." — Ephesians 5:15-16

Prudence Earns Your Rest

Just like Spyridon, a prudent shepherd, you earn your peace. Wise choices create order and safety for your 'flock'—your responsibilities and well-being.

This allows genuine free time to relax, recharge, and enjoy life without constant worry.

Prudence ensures your rest is truly restful and healthy.

Shepherd's Habits, Stronger Flock

Just as a shepherd consistently checks his flock and patrols his pastures, building strong habits is crucial for your inner scaffolding.

Your self-rules–like 'always Pause & Predict before posting' or 'Debrief after every big decision'–are like the daily routines that keep your 'flock' of choices safe and healthy.

Regular checks build reliable strength.

Your Inner Scaffolding Check-in: Building Strength

This isn't a test; it's your personal progress report! Use these questions to thoughtfully gauge your growth, celebrate your wise choices, and intentionally keep building the strong inner scaffolding that supports you through life.

Regularly pausing to reflect like this is a powerful act of prudence in itself, helping you see how far you've come and where you want to go next.

1.
On a scale of 1-5, how effectively did you use your "inner navigation app" this week? (1 = Barely used it, acted impulsively; 5 = Constantly checking, making thoughtful choices)

2.
Looking back, describe one specific wise choice you made using a skill from this manual. What was the situation? Which prudence tool did you use (e.g., Pause & Predict, Consequence Mapping, Discernment)? What was the positive outcome?

3.
Thinking about the week ahead, what is one specific Prudence skill you will intentionally focus on to strengthen your inner scaffolding? (e.g., practicing better Observation, working on Self-Correction after a misstep, seeking wise Counsel). How will you try to use it?

Learning from Ancient Paths

Spyridon, like all good shepherds, learned from generations before him.

To keep strengthening your Prudence, seek out the wisdom in ancient traditions, scriptures, and the lives of saints.

These are like old, proven maps that show where others found good pasture and avoided dangers. Their insights offer new guidance to build upon your progress.

My Field Notes & Reflections:
My Prudence Discoveries

This space is for you to be your own Investigator and Historian.

Every time you use a Prudence skill, you are making a discovery about yourself and the world.

Don't just list what happened; explain what you learned.

Not enough space? Use looseleaf pages for each week, fold and stuff into this Handbook.

Use these prompts to guide your reflections:

The "Aha!" Moment: Describe a situation where you chose to pause (Counsel) and predict the outcome before acting. What did you notice that others might have missed?

The Right-Way Challenge: Detail a choice where you picked the hard right over the easy wrong (Judgment). What made that choice so difficult, and what was the positive result?

The Course Correction: Did you make a mistake this week? That's okay! Use this space to honestly explain what went wrong and how you adapted your approach (Command). What is your new plan?

Wisdom Observed: Write down a specific action or piece of advice you saw from your Wisdom Seeker this week. What Prudence skill were they demonstrating?

About Our Saint

Saint Spyridon (c. 270 – c. 348)
was a shepherd and a bishop
from the island of Cyprus.

His life was marked by
humility, love for others, and a
deep wisdom that came from
his simple life and careful
observation.

He was known for his
miraculous deeds and his
powerful defense of the
Christian faith.

From a simple man who
learned the virtues by watching
his flock, he became a pillar of
wisdom and a guide for all who
seek to live prudently.

Final Benediction

May the wisdom of the Fathers and
the patient example of St. Spyridon
remain with you.

Go forth, not with sudden impulse,
but with the prudence you have
learned to cultivate.

May your Counsel be diligent,
your Judgment be true, and your
Command be courageous.

Remember always that the greatest
fortification you can build is the one
that lies within your own soul.

Guard your character, and your
choices will guard your life.

Amen.

www.ingramcontent.com/pod-product-compliance
Lightning Source LLC
Chambersburg PA
CBHW020824150626
46554CB00018B/2383